Foreword

This collection is a welcome example of the conversations that we need more of, and in ever greater depth across a broad range of interfaces within society, academia, government, and grassroots activism of all stripes. Crafted in response to the Mindfulness Initiative's monograph *Mindfulness: Developing Agency in Urgent Times*, these essays are themselves instances of agency, advancing the perspectives of thoughtful individuals committed to bringing greater wisdom and compassion into the world through their respective professions, passions, and perspectives on mindfulness. The world needs a lot more of this, as broadly disseminated as possible. It also needs an ever-deepening inquiry into what we mean by *agency* itself, and how it relates to mindfulness as both a formal meditation practice and as a way of being. Here the deepest questioning of all concerns the nature of self and the potential for liberation from our endemic proclivity for "selfing," in which we habitually place our own perceived interests and wellbeing above that of others.

This collection offers us at least glimmers of what an alternative might be... an agency in which our awareness is recognized as boundless, and mindfulness and compassion as the two wings of the one bird of humanity's potential for expressing embodied wakefulness and wisdom at every level of our one planetary abode. Quite the challenge for us as individuals and as a species. But the urgency and stakes are high enough for us to prioritize this kind of inquiry and conversation, and the practices that underpin their promise both individually and in intersecting communities of all kinds. Bravo to the Mindfulness Initiative for catalyzing and curating this ever-widening conversation.

Jon Kabat-Zinn
Northampton, Massachusetts
June 21, 2021

Contents

1. **Urgent times need critical, real-world research** – By Dr Rachel Lilley 4

2. **Why am I seeing this?** – By Menka Sanghvi 7

3. **Agency as Freedom** – By Chivonne Preston 10

4. **Reclaiming Sangha to transform self, society and racial injustice** – By Dr Tina Basi, PhD 12

5. **Why we need Social Mindfulness** – By Mark Leonard 14

6. **Mindfulness in higher education: awareness, knowledge and action through intentional agency** – By Dr Caroline Barratt, PhD 16

7. **The role of agency within health, and health within agency** – By Dr Karen E. Neil MRPharmSGB, MIHPE 18

8. **Why mindfulness needs to be part of (and is not sufficient for) addressing the current societal crises** – By Dusana Dorjee, PhD 20

9. **The case for compassion as another 'foundational capacity'** – By Francesca Boomsma 22

10. **The mindful reflexive self: calling for an interdisciplinary exploration of how reflexivity and mindfulness can promote agency and social change** – By Amanda Powell 24

11. **Mindfulness on the frontlines** – By Richard Reoch 26

    References 28

Please support our work

The Mindfulness Initiative doesn't receive any public funding and in order to retain its neutral and trusted advisory position in the sector cannot generate revenue from competitive products or services. As such, we are entirely dependent on philanthropic gifts for sustaining our work. If you find this discussion paper helpful, please consider making a contribution. Visit www.themindfulnessinitiative.org/appeal/donate to make a one-time or recurring donation – alternatively, get in touch.

Edited by Jamie Bristow

Editorial assistance from Marion Thackwray, Pilar Puig and Luke Fortmann. Design by J-P Stanway.

Copyright © 2021 The Mindfulness Initiative,
Sheffield, S1, United Kingdom
The Mindfulness Initiative is a Charitable Incorporated Organisation, registered number: 1179834 (England & Wales)

How to cite:

Bristow, J. (Ed.). (2021). Responding to Mindfulness: Developing Agency in Urgent Times - A compilation of essays. The Mindfulness Initiative.

Author, initial. (2021). Title of essay. In J. Bristow (Ed.), Responding to Mindfulness: Developing Agency in Urgent Times - A compilation of essays. The Mindfulness Initiative.

RESPONSE 1

Urgent times need critical, real-world research

To give mindfulness a truly transformative agency

BY DR RACHEL LILLEY

Rachel Lilley is a behaviour change expert, working with wicked problems such as climate change. She has worked on social and environmental change for over 25 years. She is co-author of *Neuroliberalism, behavioural government in the 21st Century*. She is a mindfulness and yoga teacher, and has been acclaimed for her world leading research on decision-making, mindfulness and behavioural insights working with the Welsh Government in the context of their Well Being of Future Generations Act. Contact: r.lilley@bham.ac.uk, www.predictingmind.com

Mindfulness: Developing Agency in Urgent Times is both welcome and timely. The document stitches together a fragmented evidence-base to make a compelling case that, in theory, mindfulness should support collective action. However, we also need grounded, practical and rigorous research to surface the real-life barriers to change and adapt programmes to directly address the issues we find. In this paper I describe how I have done exactly that. It describes a journey which wasn't comfortable or easy and one which challenged assumptions I, and I suspect, we all carry with us about the problem 'out there' and how we use mindfulness to address it.

The authors of the agency discussion paper are agnostic about whether existing programmes are sufficient to create change. Here I make the case that training designed to do one thing in a particular context benefits from adaption in order to do something else well in another context. It is only through evidence-informed development that we can be sure mindfulness programmes are having a reliable impact on "action in our collective best interest".

I live and work in Wales where, for the past seven years, I have led practice-based action research amongst leaders in the civil service, drawing on recent new theories of bias, mind and emotion to build a contemporary approach to mindfulness as a transformative practice. The benefit of working on the ground is that new and novel outcomes emerge from grappling with the reality of a problem in situ. Complex realities demand innovation, creativity and an ability to move beyond existing thinking.

I have spent most of my 30-year career working on social and environmental issues and in recent years this has involved becoming an academic and researching the psychological, behavioural and systemic aspects of what have come to be called 'wicked' problems. In my early years as a campaigner, I, and those around me, worked with the belief that issues could be solved using an 'information deficit approach'. In short, if the 'correct' facts were made available to people, they would then do the 'right' actions, i.e. recycle more, drive less or work in ways that were more equitable. I spent many years trying to change the world through leaflets, campaign packs and parliamentary briefings. Through lots of trial, error and research it has become clear that multiple, diverse and counter-intuitive factors influence how people see and act in the world and having the right facts is a somewhat tiny element. We regularly behave in ways that contradict our own firmly

> **We regularly behave in ways that contradict our own firmly held beliefs. Our actions are often not rational, but are contextual and relational, designed more to keep us alive in the short term than for our own long-term good, or for the continued health of our planet.**

held beliefs. Our actions are often not rational, but are contextual and relational, designed more to keep us alive in the short term than for our own long-term good, or for the continued health of our planet.

In recent years I have become an interdisciplinary social scientist and now the social and behavioural sciences inform my work. Some research on therapeutic mindfulness suggests practices of self-regulation and compassion, included in standard courses, can mitigate climate change by changing individual habits. I believe where there is already intention and capacity, this could be true, but it is limited and fails to address what is a much, much bigger systemic problem. Many of our actions are not our own choice, but are embedded in social, cultural and economic systems. In my research I looked at how I might develop a mindfulness intervention that could positively influence systems more widely. To do that I had to change the underpinning theories used in therapeutic mindfulness and draw on more recent theories of mind, emotion and self, creating new frameworks of understanding tailored to the specific context in which I worked.

In Wales a radical piece of legislation, The Well Being of Future Generations Act 2015, requires Welsh public bodies to think about the long-term impact of their decisions, to work better with people, communities and each other, and to prevent persistent problems such as poverty, health inequalities and climate change. This requires new cultures of collaboration and decision-making. I designed and researched a 'Mindfulness-Based Behavioural Insights and Decision-Making Programme' to specifically support this work. After a couple of years of tweaking existing Mindfulness-Based Stress Reduction Programmes I had a lightbulb moment, inspired through a talk by anthropologist Jo Cook where she asked: 'if mindfulness is the answer, what is the problem?'. I realised I had spent too much time adapting a pre-configured mindfulness 'solution' and not put enough effort into really understanding the nature of the problem on the ground. This, I have come to believe, is an essential piece of work needed, in research contexts, to develop more transformative mindfulness training.

I used action-based participative research methods, based on understandings of complexity and systems. This included collecting and analysing narratives to understand the problems faced by senior civil servants in Welsh Government. What became obvious was the significant change in the civil service role over the last 30 years. As one shared with me, historically civil servants "counted things and told people what to do", now they navigate high volumes of conflicting and complex information, interact with diverse stakeholders and attempt to integrate difference to co-create effective policy interventions. This requires excellent capacities of attention, perception and emotion and an understanding of how prior experience and cognitive biases filter information. The problem is civil servants and politicians lack these essential capacities needed to deal with the complexity and uncertainty they regularly face. This is mainly because they have absolutely no training on anything to do with their embodied mind, the nervous system and how as a collective we perceive and make sense of the world.

I use football (soccer) as an analogy. In the 80s in the UK the game was seen as simply technique, trained through practising drills. Success was not viewed as dependent on psychology or nutrition. Wind forward forty years and attention is given to every bit of a Premier League footballer's body and mind so that, in that key moment, they can kick the ball in exactly the right direction with perfect force. Our civil servants and politicians are needing to make fast decisions quickly, assess a complex field, negotiate and collaborate with others. To do this they use their thoughts, their nervous systems, their internal felt states and yet, when asked, they know nothing about the mechanism or influence of any of these aspects of their decision-making. Indeed the data showed that most of what civil servants 'know' about their minds and internal state is wrong, based on misinformation and their own limited folk psychologies. This includes believing that attention is unlimited, that emotions should be suppressed, that their view of others and the world out there is largely accurate, rather than filtered and framed according to internal models and biases.

This undoubtedly leads to poorer decisions, less effective collaboration, prejudice and ironically, it potentially results in mental health problems, as they become overwhelmed and experience poor interactions and relationships. Usually mindfulness is offered at this point when a wellbeing intervention is needed. It attempts to rectify the situation rather than prevent it, helping people understand their mind and internal state once there is a problem, in other words, shutting the door once the horse has bolted.

The MBBI programme was designed informed by this in-situ analysis of the problem. The course aimed to create a culture of better decision-making and collaboration, a side effect was it helped avoid the negative impacts of stress and mental health issues. To develop the programme I explored new research on the links between cognition and emotion and current scientific challenges to the evolutionary monkey mind, the default mode network and the function of the amygdala, all of which underpin standard MBSR/CT programmes. I introduced and tested theories of mind and emotions which situated our embodied selves as emerging from our relationships and context, also as more predictive in nature rather than reactive stimulus-response machines. Interestingly this aligns with progressive social models of health emerging in some areas of public health.

The result was surprisingly successful. Managers reported changing the way they listened to each other and their teams, shifting their management style to one that was more collaborative, where they were regularly challenging their own biases and assumptions and more open to different perspectives. No

> **As the Mindfulness Initiative discussion paper suggests, we urgently need rigorous research which draws more widely on the social sciences, not just psychology. This will shed new light on underlying problems and create approaches that don't just mindlessly adapt our pre-conceived answers, but creatively and wisely create the solutions we need.**

compassion training was included in the programme but participants become more empathetic. It seemed there had not been a lack of compassion, but rather a lack of knowledge and capacities of mind.

My research concluded that systemic change in policy making is prevented, at least in part, because politicians and civil servants do not understand the very thing they use to do their job, their own embodied minds. This is not a spiritual or a therapeutic issue, it is basic lack of education and self-awareness, something mindfulness interventions can, if designed well, do something about. If we are to use mindfulness to create urgency in these times, as the Mindfulness Initiative discussion paper suggests, we urgently need rigorous research which draws more widely on the social sciences, not just psychology. This will shed new light on underlying problems and create approaches that don't just mindlessly adapt our pre-conceived answers, but creatively and wisely create the solutions we need. •

RESPONSE 2

Why am I seeing this?

Algorithms making choices for us

BY MENKA SANGHVI

Menka Sanghvi is a multidisciplinary researcher and facilitator, working on creative projects for spreading mindfulness and compassion in contemporary contexts. Menka is the lead author of the *Fieldbook for Mindfulness Innovators* published by the Mindfulness Initiative, Director of Learning at Mind Over Tech's digital habits academy, and the creator of a mindful photography club, *Just Looking*. Contact: me@menkasanghvi.com, Menkasanghvi.com

There's a lot about our digital lives that makes us feel that we're not in control. An hour can pass by in oblivion, before we realise that we didn't mean to be on our phones for quite so long. And as with all habits, the more we engage with our devices in this way, the harder it becomes to stop. In order to regain more personal autonomy, the authors of *Mindfulness: Developing Agency In Urgent Times* stress the importance of actively making conscious choices about what we pay attention to. A resounding yes! But I also worry about the number of decisions that are already made for us, long before we get to them.

> **Yes, we're still in charge, but the algorithms influence us at every step.**

Behind the scenes and screens, nearly all the information we see online is filtered for us by algorithms that carefully pre-arrange our choices for us. Almost everything we see is a "recommendation": friends, news, adverts, movies, clothes, jobs and more. No two people see the same content because the internet is increasingly personalised based on demographics and past activity, made up of thousands of data points. Even search engines customise results based on who's asking. Yes, we're still in charge, but the algorithms influence us at every step.

This, in itself, is no bad thing. Given the streams of information we wade through online, it would be difficult to navigate without the help of intermediaries paring down our options. It has a healthy precedent too. Historically, we have relied upon trusted curators, advisers, and gatekeepers to make sense of the world. Thanks to machine learning, the robots assisting us today know us better than our closest confidants. Perhaps, even better than we know ourselves. It can feel good to be so well understood, to have someone by our side, finishing off our sentences.

The trouble with this cosy arrangement is that our relationship is not really with the machines, but rather with the people that create them. Filtering algorithms are imbued with a purpose, based on a business model. These are motivated not just to read our minds, but also to change our minds. The goal of social media platforms is to engage us in adverts. The goal of online shops is to have us buy more. The goal of some news portals is to change our political allegiance. These agendas - rarely stated upfront - are not objectively good or bad, but likely to be in conflict with our own.

I once tried to find out the actual criteria used by Facebook to curate my news feed, but it's a safely guarded secret. Elsewhere, complex algorithms are simply treated as black boxes that can't be understood entirely. However, there is a popular industry term - "relevance" - that keeps coming up in describing

> **We stand to lose our common reference points, and empathy for each other's reality. In prioritising so-called relevant content, everything else slips away into the background.**

personalisation algorithms. As Mark Zuckerberg of Facebook explained: "A squirrel dying in front of your house may be more relevant to your interests right now than people dying in Africa."[1] Relevance in this context is not the same as, say, usefulness, or importance. It is simply what will engage you in the behaviour that the platform wants for you, or *from* you.

So what's at stake here? Well, for one thing, we stand to lose our common reference points, and empathy for each other's reality. In prioritising so-called relevant content, everything else slips away into the background. And the more limited our worldview, the more vulnerable we become to polarisation. Technology activist Eli Pariser coined the term "filter bubbles" to describe this phenomenon.[2] Others call it an "'echo chamber" in which you can only hear your own voice. These metaphors point to an underlying crisis: a disconnection from other people and their perspectives.

On these private islands, all our biases and preferences are strengthened and solidified. The algorithm observes, for example, any negativity bias that inclines us towards reading and sharing negative news. It observes the confirmation bias that draws us towards content that concurs with our existing beliefs. It notes our taste for certain kinds of movies or music. And because historical data is diligently baked into our profiles, past choices influence our present options, making it harder to make different choices now. Harder to change and grow as people. In this way, data shapes our destiny.

Mindfulness practice can help disentangle us from these forces, because it enables us step back from automatic behaviours and act with intention. Capacities such as awareness, decentering and cognitive flexibility are instrumental in avoiding the automations described. But I'm wondering: how might we need to expand and adapt our mindfulness practices to meet this new challenge more directly? Here are some ideas.

- **Noticing our virtual selves.**
  We need mindfulness not just of our minds and bodies, but also of the structure of our lives in terms of our informational landscape and relationship with technology. We could go so far as to say that in addition to being physical, psychological and social beings we are also technological beings, and the online informational spaces we inhabit can be mindfully observed and inquired into as an extension of ourselves. Perhaps we need a digital equivalent of a body scan.

- **Studying our own biases.**
  It has become the norm for technology companies to hire psychologists and neuroscientists into their teams, and user experience designers are trained in cognitive biases. If we want to understand how this new world of algorithms impacts us, we too need to get to know our biases better. A simple starting point is to examine the personalised content on our screens. At times the mirror won't be totally accurate, but at other times the algorithms may have picked up on some unconscious biases that we ourselves have yet to acknowledge.

- **Clicking 'out loud'.**
  When every click, swipe and play is tracked and has a consequence, clicking becomes a lot like speaking out loud. Treating our clicks as an external expression could make us more cautious, and if we did regret engaging with specific content, for instance, a conspiracy theory video, we might make the effort to set the record straight. Some actions can be deleted or undone, such as a Google Search history or an Instagram like. We could also deliberately click on the opposite kind of content to recalibrate. Because, if we don't clear up a misunderstanding, the algorithms won't know that we didn't really mean it.

- **Radical, mindful curiosity.**
  When was the last time you saw something truly surprising online? When everything starts to look familiar, there is nothing more to learn. If we don't want to be trapped in a stale information landscape we must diversify what we search for, who we follow, and what we click on. This requires an epistemic humility and mindful curiosity. Every time we actively get curious about a different culture, ideology or perspective, we retrain the algorithms, creating a positive feedback loop.

- **Adding friction by design.**
  A habit is an action that has become so easy, so frictionless, that conscious intention and willpower are no longer required. If we want to change our digital habits we need to make some actions much harder for ourselves, inviting our brain's executive control function to get involved. For example, by simply switching off the autoplay function on Youtube we create a mindful pause after one video has ended, giving us an opportunity to reconnect with our intentions.

- **Being more private.**
  While we may not be able to switch off tracking and filtering entirely, there are a number of steps we can each take to increase the anonymity of our behaviours online, such that our web experience does not become as tightly personalised. For example, switching off the customisation feature in Google Search or going on YouTube "incognito" will expand what we see, and diversify our possibilities.

All these responses rely on individual action, and there's a risk here of misplacing burden. We also need to lobby collectively for structural changes including regulations for companies and government bodies that employ algorithms, asking them to provide greater transparency, accountability and controls in how their algorithms are trained, and how they make decisions about, and for, us.

> **Mindfulness may not be able to defend us from these kinds of distortions of our reality, but it will certainly give us more of a fighting chance to protect some parts of our inner lives from the influence of machines.**

If you're still on the fence about how important this is, let me leave you with a near-future scenario to consider. Imagine wearing glasses that visually prioritise or recommend certain people as you walk down the road - reinforcing your own biases, or worse, marketing a third-party political or commercial agenda. Certain people, more "relevant" ones perhaps, might appear brighter or more vivid in this augmented reality, offering you a tailored experience of the physical world.

Anyone who has tried to meditate knows how fundamental, but difficult, it is to remain detached from thoughts, and to treat thoughts as mental events rather than facts. But when our thoughts are driven by our visual sense, it is extremely hard not to "believe our eyes". Mindfulness may not be able to defend us from these kinds of distortions of our reality, but it will certainly give us more of a fighting chance to protect some parts of our inner lives from the influence of machines.

RESPONSE 3

Agency as Freedom

BY CHIVONNE PRESTON MSC, MA, ACA

Chivonne Preston is the CEO of Mindfulness in Schools Project (MiSP), a charity providing world-leading curricula for classroom-based mindfulness and delivering training and support to its broad community of teachers. MiSP's work focuses on giving both adults and children in schools the skills to manage and maintain their own wellbeing, developing connections with themselves and with each other so that teaching and learning can flourish. Contact: chivonne.preston@mindfulnessinschools.org

What does it mean to be 'developing agency' in urgent times? This essay briefly examines the inimitable relationship between the 'individual and collective capacity for intentional action'[3], as described in *Mindfulness: Developing Agency in Urgent Times*, and the concept of freedom. It concludes that 'developing agency' in fact corresponds to empowering ourselves, which is particularly relevant for children and young people upon whose shoulders this urgency is piling.

Freedom comes in many forms which you could spend a lifetime studying[4]: freedom of thought, expression, speech, action, movement, assembly, and so on. For many, the COVID-19 pandemic has brought these into sharp focus as citizens are told to stay at home, avoid each other, and wear masks. We notice our freedom when we no longer have it — and perhaps in noticing our constraints[5] we best recognise, and can then employ, our freedoms.

Noticing constraints is a fascinating practice. Take a moment, now, to consider: what is stopping you from planting a tree? From making a donation to a worthy cause? From visiting a global landmark? From speaking up on social media about the issues you care about?

Constraints on our behaviour are usually physical, financial, or social. Whilst the last of these includes group norms such as the systems of law, education, and social interaction, it also contains psychological constraints that impede individual or collective action and which can be both conscious and unconscious: morality, desire, but also inertia and fear. There is a growing body of work exploring typically concealed psychological constraints such as our race, gender and age bias[6], helping us understand our individual contexts[7] and, therefore, the predispositions which also enslave us. And we now recognise the hazardous potential of the 'attention economy' to increase both inertia and the shackle of desire[8].

> **Put simply: by being alert to that which is preventing us from acting, we unlock for ourselves greater freedom to act, and can acquire the skills and power to do so.**

There is a great deal written about the potential of mindfulness to help us notice and step out of our 'autopilot' and habits of mind and body in order to gain 'sufficient freedom... to enact measures that reduce the difficulty'[9] — i.e., to find courage and confidence to choose our next actions despite our fears and conditioning. But there is, I believe, still further scope to consider how mindfulness can aid us in (1) proactively identifying constraints, whichever type they may be, (2) unpicking our relationship to both conscious and unconscious constraints to help us identify our own personal 'values' (i.e. 'figure out what to do' as described in *Mindfulness: Developing Agency in Urgent Times*), and therefore (3) increasing the potential we have for individual and collective action. Put simply: by being alert to that which is preventing us from acting, we unlock for ourselves greater freedom to act, and can acquire the skills and power to do so.

In his superb analysis of the threat of climate change and civilisational collapse, Tim Gorringe proposes that when we can recognise that 'fear simply paralyses' and the 'hedonism of contemporary society is a form of displacement activity' where pleasure has become an addiction, we can choose an alternative path. He calls for 'revolutionary humanism' rooted in an alternative value and virtue system lived and practised both individually and collectively[10].

This notion of 'living by our values' is not new. Indeed, it was once the standard rationale for government[11] and is common parlance in the corporate world[12] where business advisers laud the relationship between values and action. Answering 'What are my values? How can I live them?' is more difficult in a modern world without consistent 'value leadership' and public discussion.

And the risk is that it is easier to pay lip service to the mindfulness values of curiosity, non-judgment, kindness, compassion, and so on than it is to correlate these values with our own actual individual and collective lived actions. As mindfulness practitioners well know, living mindfully is hard! It is difficult because the application and integration of the practice of mindfulness into our everyday lives — applying it to both our action and our inaction — cannot happen unless we are aware of ourselves and our environment: and thereby aware of our values and the constraints to living them.

> **Mindfulness enables both the teacher and the student to notice their own constraints, to identify their own values, to engage in dialogue, and to recognise the freedom and the impetus they have to act, both individually and collectively.[14]**

So what does this mean for these 'urgent times'? Current projections predict 'peak human' at the end of this century[13]. How can we 'tool up' humanity to overcome the constraints of habit, inertia, fear, and incessant distraction to empower our own freedom to respond to this escalating urgency? The answer, as recognised by both liberators and enslavers[14], lies in education.

Much as the liberation philosophers from 1960s South America heralded the role of education[15] and cooperation in restoring humanity from oppression, my view is that we must educate individuals in the 21st century so that we all have tools to liberate ourselves from the constraints that prevent us from acting. Mindfulness enables both the teacher and the student to notice their own constraints, to identify their own values, to engage in dialogue, and to recognise the freedom and the impetus they have to act, both individually and collectively[16]. Teachers and students welcome this opportunity because it is relevant to them and their world.

It is in this empowerment that the development of agency rests. That is why mindfulness lessons should be offered to every adult and every child, now, before it is too late.

RESPONSE 4

Reclaiming Sangha to transform self, society and racial injustice

BY DR TINA BASI, BA, MA, PHD

Tina Basi is a Sociologist at the LSE and the University of Cambridge. She teaches the MBCT/MBSR courses and is working with the Mindfulness Project on mindfulness and racial awareness. Tina also co-leads the RSA's Mindful Living Network where she is working on the role of community and society in contemporary mindfulness practices. Contact: t.basi@lse.ac.uk

We are indeed living in urgent times. At the point of writing, the grip of the pandemic is yet to loosen and still, as creatures of progress, we find ourselves considering ways in which we can move forward. The authors of *Mindfulness: Developing Agency in Urgent Times*, quite rightly point out that mindfulness is no silver bullet or "topical cure for society's ills, but a way of *being* in relationship with the world which supports agency: our individual and collective capacity for intentional action" [emphasis added].[17] They argue that evidence-based mindfulness can be a resource in bringing about a step change in society.

Whilst we can recognise the urgency in creating necessary social change, for example, by addressing racial injustice, how can we better engage with the notion of agency? The authors write, "agency depends heavily upon… directing our attention purposefully in line with personal goals."[18] Yet they also recognise that social change comes about vis-à-vis a dynamic process between individual and society. "It is in groups and through an inherently social, dialectic process that we develop knowledge and test our understanding."[19] Ultimately, in order for mindfulness to be a resource in bringing about necessary social change, one must be willing to do the 'inner' work experienced in a sustained practice, and the 'outer' work of taking action, both as an individual and as part of a collective.

What is meant by a collective? Is it social movements? Policy makers? Wider society? What happens when our individual goals are in conflict with necessary social change?

Throughout the literature on contemporary mindfulness the Sanskrit term 'sangha' is invariably described as community or congregation. In root wisdom traditions it is thought to be a necessary context for personal transformation. How can we begin to conceive of 'sangha' in the call to action the authors set out? Where can we find these communities of meditators and social change makers? More importantly, why has 'sangha' been separated from individual mindfulness practices when so many of the world's cultures and societies see the transformation of individual and the community as intertwined, whether that be through meditation, hymn singing, prayer, or acts of community service? The modernising of mindfulness has been useful in secularizing practices and in creating greater accessibility but this has come at a cost.

There is a long and documented history of traditions and practices moving from east to west, and in doing so, undergoing a process of colonization. At a conceptual level, the process of colonizing is problematic enough, but when addressing race and racial injustice within the world of secular mindfulness it becomes even more complex. Firstly, the process has separated the individual and the 'sangha' and secondly, mindfulness leaders, teachers, authors, and practitioners are predominantly white.

The colonizing of mindfulness has marred both process and purpose – process because we have lost 'sangha' and purpose because without 'sangha' we will struggle to do the work of anti-racism. As a critique emerges of the whiteness of the sector and its whitewashing (altering something in a way that caters to white people), we must all ask ourselves what role we can play in the decolonizing of mindfulness.[20] In part, we ought to stop cherry picking the things we like and instead spend time learning about the wider contexts and origins of mindfulness practices. We know that decolonising is not merely a project of discourse; thus decolonising includes the reclaiming of 'sangha'.[21] Increasing the evidence base of mindfulness research to extend to Black, Indigenous, People of Colour (BIPOC) is also an act of decolonising mindfulness.

What *Mindfulness: Developing Agency in Urgent Times* is calling for is social change. When we are looking at racism, however, we cannot only begin at the level of the individual. This is because racism and racialised discourses are located within a complex web of white supremacy.[22] Socially unacceptable white supremacy is easily identified with examples of Nazism and the Ku Klux Klan, however the implicit belief that white people are superior to others and acts such as cultural appropriation and white-saviour complex are often not so easily recognised as part of the racist social structure within which we all live and participate. It is precisely because of this lack of acute awareness that I suggest agency, with respect to anti-racism, must begin in relation to the collective, to 'sangha'.

The authors outline three fruitful ways in which mindfulness can intersect with ways of "being in relationship with the world."[23] Section One, "Perception", can be utilised to reframe the information we are absorbing. Ruth King has written that what people of colour really need is for white people to wake up to their own whiteness and the document notes that "heightened capacity for perspective was a recurrent theme" from MBCT participants.[24, 25]

> **Agency alone cannot bring about social change. It is merely potential and can only be understood relationally to structure.**

Section Two, "Understanding", can be utilised as an opportunity to educate or 'do the work'. This section looks at the ways in which "mindful awareness integrates thinking into an intuitive, embodied experience of the world"[26] ... the body supplies an endless stream of subtle signals... a subtle, embodied navigation system.[27] Thus our learning is born not only out of our minds or books we read but also out of our embodied experiences, of living and being with others.

Section Three, "Doing," has the most to offer when engaging with anti-racism as it includes a discussion of the tension between 'doing' and 'being mode'. This is really where the journey of anti-racism begins. The authors point out that, "misaligned actions can effectively cancel out each other's effect."[28] Yes, mindfulness training cultivates greater empathy and compassion for those in distress, but we must be wary of fixing "things before we understand."[29] White allyship (acting in solidarity)[30] is fraught with white privilege (having unearned benefits as a result of being white)[31] and 'doing' without enough 'being' has resulted in problematic outcomes such as tokenism, colour blindness, or white saviourism for example.

Agency alone cannot bring about social change. It is merely potential and can only be understood relationally to structure. We all live within structures and dynamic flows of power that shape our identities, practices, and lifestyles.[32] It has been written elsewhere that, "on an internal level, racism is found to be rooted in a delusion of a false sense of self... structural racism, ethnocentricism, and colonialism are external manifestations of this existential condition".[33] Such observations call upon us to recognise that experiences of agency differ across class, race, ethnicity, gender, and socio-economic positions to name a few. What better way to engage with such differences than through deeper fostering and flourishing of 'sangha'? 'Sangha', quite simply, offers us the inclusive space within which we can embark on the inner and outer work of social justice.

RESPONSE
5

Why we need Social Mindfulness

BY MARK LEONARD

Mark Leonard, Director/Lead Practitioner, Mindfulness Connected
Mark has always worked for a sustainable future. He believes that 'social mindfulness' provides the key to developing organisational culture that can meet the challenges of our times. He helped to establish the Oxford Mindfulness Centre, and, using Mindfulness-based Cognitive Therapy as scaffolding, evolved an interactive approach to understanding mindfulness as a social process in organisations.
Contact: mark@mindfulnessconnected.com

At the beginning of the last century, Alfred Stieglitz took a photograph of an artwork his friend submitted for an exhibition in New York, which he described like this: "Everyone who has seen it thinks it beautiful—And it's true—it is. It has an oriental look about it—a cross between a Buddha and a veiled woman."

This artwork wasn't exhibited and the original was lost, yet today you can see reproductions in museums in cities across the world. If you do see one of them, there will be a soundscape of whispers and squeaking shoes. You will see a smooth, white curved form in a transparent box on a white plinth. Even though you are now looking at a reproduction of the artwork that Stieglitz described a hundred years ago, it is more than likely that it will not remind you of a Buddha or veiled woman at all.

Talking about impressions people have about this artwork is the first activity in a 'social mindfulness' programme, which was originally developed for the Royal Orthopaedic Hospital in Birmingham to release the power of individual and collective agency, one mindful conversation at a time. One female member of staff from the hospital thought it was a fruit bowl. Another thought it was a bedpan. All the men thought they knew what it was, but only some of them were right.

Stieglitz is actually describing what its creator termed a readymade work of art, which critics have voted the most influential artwork of the 20th century. It was originally made to be fixed to a wall and plumbed into the drains, in a gentleman's public toilet. Marcel Duchamp bought it from J.L. Mott Iron Works and daubed "R Mutt, 1917" on it, and entitled it Fountain. If you see one of its reproductions in a museum, your eyes will see light reflected from the same form as everyone else, but what you think it is will be shaped by social sensibilities, expectations, and memories, all determined by social conditioning from your past. At first sight this truth may seem unremarkable, but there's more to it than meets the eye.

Social mindfulness programmes use group activities, like the one described above, as a learning process to understand how different people experience things differently, and to create a sense of trust in the group. The sense of social safety created by sharing thoughts and feelings also helps people to feel comfortable before closing their eyes and focusing attention on bodily sensations in mindfulness meditation, in the company of others. And then, meditating together deepens feelings of trust, safety, and connection in the group. People take these insights, conversational skills, and feelings with them into the workplace, organisation, or community in which they belong.

Around the time that Duchamp triggered a revolution in the artworld, a Burmese monk, Ledi Sayadaw, taught that directly observing experience was a shortcut to understanding Buddhist truths. He created a quick method to make it possible for lay Buddhists to become teachers of the Dhamma (wisdom teachings) during a time of change. While Duchamp changed the way we understand the function of art in society, Ledi Sayadaw made mindfulness a readymade approach that was later repurposed as a tool to manage the stress of modern life.

Like Marcel Duchamp's readymade, mindfulness meditation has been transplanted from one context into another. Both also help us gain insight into the way we create our own private realities out of thoughts and feelings. Understanding how we do this can help us to see ourselves and the world around us in new ways. How does this help us tackle the challenges of our times?

The Mindfulness Initiative's new document, *Mindfulness: Developing Agency in Urgent Times*, reframes the context of mindfulness to explore how it might address contemporary social and environmental challenges. Reflecting the current evidence base, the document mainly focuses on the benefits of individual mindfulness practice and how these can give us some capacity for autonomy and agency in our lives. The intention of this essay is to develop this theme to explore how we might need to reperceive mindfulness as an intervention that is explicitly repurposed to bring about social and organisational change. I believe, this requires a shift from thinking about ourselves as individuals, to understand our humanness as something that is inextricably intertwined with the way we, collectively, understand ourselves, relate to each other, and think about the world around us. Recognising these differences in framing makes it possible to design a new approach to mindfulness that is intended to help us understand how we, collectively, can go about making more human organisations and a better world.

The maxim I am not my brother's keeper frees us from any concerns we may have about the way our self-serving behaviour may affects others. The modern miracle is built on rights and responsibilities: personal freedom; responsibility to provide for ourselves; and enjoyment of our property and the fruits of our labour. These rights and responsibilities encourage self-reliance and the entrepreneurial spirit, creating wealth and opportunity. There have been huge benefits to economic development, but there are also costs: stress, inequality, loss of community, wasteful consumption, and environmental destruction.

We have replaced our human need for intimacy and community with an obsession with outward signs of success. We have come to understand the human mind as a collection of psychological processes. In this context, mindfulness becomes a self-help tool that can free us from our emotional distress, enabling us to carry on with business as usual. Critics of this approach argue that this doesn't do anything about the causes of our condition, it just makes things worse.

However, mindfulness doesn't just regulate our emotions, it gives us a sense of perspective that enables us to come back to our senses… It helps us to reconnect with our emotions, which are at the heart of our human experience and, with sufficient dedication to practising it, it can even help us rediscover the intrinsic value of friendliness, kindness, and love. Could mindfulness foster these human qualities to create a just society and reduce consumption to levels that enable us to reverse climate change?

> **It takes a critical mass of individuals working together, winning hearts and minds.**

Even if mindfulness enables us to live more meaningful lives, our capacity for agency as individuals is limited because so much of our behaviour is controlled by forces outside our control. Change at an organisational or social level requires more than this. It takes a critical mass of individuals working together, winning hearts and minds.

This is why we need social mindfulness to bring about the kind of social, economic, and environmental changes we must make: We learn from each other in conversations where we can share our thoughts and feelings without fear of rejection or exclusion. Understanding our differences builds trust and makes it possible for us to share our different strengths. We recognise the impact our behaviour has on others. We extend our sense of identity to include others. We understand that our interests are inseparable from those of others. We align ourselves, individually and collectively, with the greater good, and organise ourselves to meet everyone's needs.

RESPONSE 6

Mindfulness in higher education

Awareness, knowledge and action through intentional agency

BY DR CAROLINE BARRATT, PHD

Caroline Barratt is Deputy Director of Education in the School of Health and Social Care, University of Essex and founder of the Contemplative Pedagogy Network. She is an experienced meditator, mindfulness teacher and has a particular interest in contemplative pedagogy for staff and students in higher education. Contact: barrattc@essex.ac.uk

Mindfulness: Developing Agency in Urgent Times has succinctly outlined a conceptual framework for how mindfulness may help to address the complex issues of our time by supporting 'intentional action.' As an educator, in this response I want to use the lens of agency to highlight the value of mindfulness and contemplative practice in higher education.

Education and culture are intricately woven. The things that we teach our children and young people shape society and either enhance or constrain our capacity to effectively respond to the challenges that we face. The ethics and values expressed within society are reflected implicitly and explicitly in what and how we teach. Currently, education has a strong bias towards teaching objective knowledge, providing information and facts about the world that lies 'out there'. Within higher education, there is much emphasis placed on developing the cognitive domain of students and helping them become 'critical thinkers' whose agency is understood as their ability to interpret the evidence in front of them. The ideal is to be as objective as possible with little space given for the subjective, embodied and emotional experience of being human or for understanding the limits of that objectivity.

The complementary and interconnected innovations of mindfulness in education and 'contemplative pedagogy' have brought this imbalance, this neglect of what Ergas (2017) refers to as the 'inner curriculum', more clearly into view.[34] Contemplative pedagogy 'shifts the focus of teaching and learning to incorporate "first person" approaches which connect students to their lived, embodied experience of their own learning'.[35] It rebalances modern education's bias towards objective knowledge of the external world by valuing the subjective and actively drawing that out into the classroom. The introduction of mindfulness practice in education has meant that our minds themselves, not just the world they perceive, have been put on the curriculum. Ergas (2017: 6) notes:

'Ignoring the mind as the other half of the "curriculum", "education" becomes a hall of mirrors in which "society" educates the mind to mirror back its own ways of thinking...'

Using a model of individual and collective agency with three domains of perceiving, understanding and doing, the paper shows how mindfulness practice facilitates exploration of the interplay between the subjective, internal world and objective, external world. The authors argue that agency does not just depend upon understanding the contents of mind but also upon seeing more clearly the mind itself and appreciating how the mind determines our experience, sense of meaning and values. As well as highlighting the importance of mindfulness, this interplay points to a foundational role for contemplative education more broadly, in which learning how the mind works becomes as important as what we use it for.

> **With its focus on objectivity and reason, present-day education fails to educate us about the gap between ethical intentions and actual behaviour.**

The first domain of the agency model, 'perceiving', describes the potential of mindfulness practice to make us aware of — and help us to exercise choice over — where we place our attention. Attention is crucial for effective agency. Students are often being asked to engage in challenging tasks that may feel uncomfortable, leading to procrastination and mind-wandering. The capacity to bring attention back to the task at hand, despite difficulty, is crucial for educational success as well as living a life of purpose and meaning. The 'internal climate of friendliness' that mindfulness practice helps to cultivate develops the capacity of students to hold 'not knowing' and develop an openness to new ideas that may challenge their understanding of the world.

The second section, on 'understanding', illustrates how mindfulness practice may support us in dealing with the volume of often contradictory information to which we are exposed. Within higher education, mindfulness may support students to hold the complexity of the world from a decentred perspective, preventing them from getting stuck in entrenched positions that impede collective learning and action. Given that it is often university graduates who are trying to solve complex, intricate and serious problems, education needs to enable students to hold the bigger picture, the 'coherent, dynamic whole' (page 21), along with an understanding of the parts, rather than simply argue for one viewpoint or another.

Under the third domain of the model, 'Doing', it is possible to draw out how mindfulness training can help support and enrich aspects of education that may be already present but need development. For example, I remember being taught to be kind in school. But I wasn't taught how or, crucially, what I should do when I feel like doing something selfish or unkind. With its focus on objectivity and reason, present-day education fails to educate us about the gap between ethical intentions and actual behaviour. Humans are conceptualised as rational decision-makers weighing up the evidence and acting in accordance with that evidence. This detached perspective doesn't allow room for our emotional, embodied experience as human beings, and as such, students are not sensitive to their own contradictions and those of others, and as such, their capacity to live ethically in the world is impinged. The practice of mindfulness cultivates an allowing space in which these incongruities can be explored and the impact they may have on others and our collaborative work examined.

The paper has helped to make clearer how mindfulness practice can contribute to social change through education. The model of agency provides a useful springboard for thinking about the kind of skills and capacities we want graduates to have. For societies to change, education must also change. However, to elicit these potential benefits, it is not sufficient for mindfulness to be taught as an add-on to education. It must be integrated, moving from what Ergas and Hadar (2019) describe as mindfulness in education to mindfulness as education.[36]

How can this be done? Within higher education (HE), the purpose of the university is currently under question, and rapid social and economic change means that preparing students for the future is very difficult.[37] A focus on critical thinking has long been the cornerstone of a university education, but it doesn't make room for the embodied and complex experience of human life. Additionally, HE is increasingly measured in relation to graduate employability and earning capacity in an environment in which education is seen as a way of accruing competitive advantage over others.[38] The overriding culture of striving, competition and achievement runs counter to the space that mindfulness opens up. Yet increasing levels of stress and anxiety amongst both students[39] and staff[40] and the loss of purpose being experienced in HE[41] create a fertile environment for new ideas about ways of working which are more human, kind and holistic.

In this context, the aspiration of developing human agency and intentional action, as presented in this paper, could inform the aims of higher education by balancing the need to learn about the external world with understanding how our minds construct and navigate that world. ●

RESPONSE 7

The role of agency within health, and health within agency

BY DR KAREN E. NEIL MRPHARMSGB, MIHPE

Karen Neil is a specialist pharmacist in health promotion and education and co-author of the textbook Disease Management. She is an experienced mindfulness teacher and supervisor. Karen recently received the GHP Health & Pharmaceutical award Most Innovative Health & Wellbeing Education Specialist 2020 (Midlands) and is a trustee with the Institute for Health Promotion and Education.
Contact: k.neil@mindfulmedicine.co.uk

It was surprising, as a young pharmacist, to see antidepressants and painkillers on a 'fast-mover' shelf, close to hand to save time. In 2018, concerns of overuse of strong painkillers, antidepressants and sleeping tablets led to a review by Public Health England[42]. A 'severe lack of alternatives' was highlighted as a reason for long-term prescribing of these drugs by GPs.[43] The impact of overuse of these drugs on a societal level, given side effects that impact decision-making, is deeply concerning, and has implications not only for health service resources, but also the required action described in *Mindfulness: Developing Agency in Urgent Times* (2020).[44]

The discussion paper by Bristow, Bell and Nixon suggests how mindfulness could be foundational to intentional action in the collective best interest. In this response, I would like to explore an overlooked element – that agency, which mindfulness underpins, is also vital for personal health and that personal health, in turn, is vital for both agency and concern about collective issues. The Zen Master, Thich Nhat Hanh, describes mindfulness training as 'medicine for our time,[45]' and there is increasing research interest in the role of mindfulness in sustainability and the connection between individual, collective and planetary wellbeing.[46]

In the West, we have long lived with the expectation of 'a pill for every ill,' and there is a tendency to depend on medicine so much that we have forgotten the extraordinary capacity of the body to heal, and the part we play in that. Even at a time when we need to take care of our health to prevent the serious impact of Coronaviruses, and to optimise our immune response to vaccines, government policy and public health guidance rarely mention the importance of self-care and how to keep our immune systems functioning well.

> **Taking care of our minds has never been more important.**

We know that stress impacts immunity, and a link has been shown between psychological factors and susceptibility to respiratory viruses[47]. Richard Davidson and his team have reported an increased antibody response to influenza vaccination following an 8-week course in Mindfulness Based Stress Reduction[48]. As such, taking care of our minds has never been more important. However, as pharmacy undergraduates we had limited teaching on the impact of nutrition on disease and even less on stress and supporting emotional health. The impact of stress on health only became apparent during my work in community pharmacy, along with the need for self-care interventions and preventative medicine. Thankfully, health professionals are now increasingly supporting patients to engage in self-care, but this depends upon their ability to act intentionally.[49]

Mindfulness course participants frequently report a sense of empowerment and a greater control over their lives. As a mindfulness teacher over the last decade, it has become increasingly clear to me that practice helps people to take care of their own health, seeing more clearly what nurtures and what is harmful and then being more able to act upon it. A gradual transition occurs from a predominantly reactive state, often described as 'automatic pilot,' to more considered responsiveness. Automatic pilot, by definition, comprises limited awareness, drawing on conditioned, well-rehearsed habits that do not always serve us well. Mindfulness introduces space for a more conscious, wiser way of living and this helps to build resilience, with evidence not only showing that expert meditators recover more quickly from stress, but also exhibit reduced expression of genes involved in inflammation.[50] There is some evidence that training reduces long-term health costs.[51]

This mechanism is most clearly at play, and with the strongest evidence of benefit, where mindfulness is used to combat harmful addiction, pain, and depression.[52] For instance, in contrast to commonly used fear-based methods, smokers are invited to smoke mindfully, often leading to repulsion through deeper noticing of the unpleasantness of the taste, smell, and discolouration of their teeth, hands, and nails. Alongside additional mindfulness practices, taught over 8 sessions, there is evidence of a sustained reduction in cigarette smoking.[53] For those who use alcohol and other substances harmful to health, often to escape from painful experiences, mindfulness offers an alternative way to cope with distress and has been shown to contribute to a reduction in risk of relapse over time.[54] Bringing compassionate presence, curiosity and receptivity to the discomfort of craving alcohol and the after-effects of impaired sleep, dehydration, depressant effects, and additional health risks from its carcinogenic metabolite, can support the decision to act differently.[55]

Mindfulness has also been shown to impact obesity, again highlighting its value in public health with reduced risk of disease through choice.[56,57] For pain, a compassionate approach with curiosity, as opposed to avoiding and fighting against it, has enabled people to titrate their own dose of painkillers, often reducing reliance on medication with adverse effects.[58,59] In depression, mindfulness is an evidence-based alternative to long-term reliance on antidepressants.[60] This approach and the resultant accumulation of clearer, richer information enabling choice and therefore change, is explored in detail in *Mindfulness: Developing Agency in Urgent Times* (2020).[44]

Given the empowerment of individuals to make positive lifestyle changes, it can be argued that mindfulness has a vital role to play in public health and disease management. Indeed, the development of 'expert patients' has been shown to improve patient outcomes through increased self-management.[61] This again brings about agency with self-care taking a greater role alongside prescribed medicines when they are needed. An increased understanding of our physiology, stress, the disease process, and treatment options, often referred to as health literacy, adds to individual wisdom and insight into often unique paths to wellbeing. Mindfulness could therefore be considered foundational to the urgent call for further investment in a 'settings approach' to public health, including health-promoting schools, hospitals, workplaces, and prisons.[62,63,64]

The development of skills to reduce stress, a major contributor to disease[65], and navigate suffering, together with building resources to strengthen wellbeing and resilience combine to reduce reliance on medication. Working with healthcare professionals to increase understanding of the risks, benefits, and appropriate use of medicines can also resource individuals to better manage their own health conditions, improving outcomes and enabling greater engagement in society, which in turn can add meaning and purpose to their lives, further benefiting wellbeing.[66]

In conclusion, mindfulness empowers us to take control of our own wellbeing and break free of unhelpful habits, ignorance and fear that lead to disease. Having the tools to respond wisely to life's challenges empowers patients and medics alike to work together, in many cases providing an alternative to high doses of medication, reducing adverse effects which can impair daily functioning and decision-making. Mindfulness compliments medicine well, helping to optimise medical intervention, alongside individualised care of our physical and emotional health, thus improving quality of life, reducing strain on health services, and increasing our capacity to act collectively to solve the crises we are facing today.

RESPONSE 8

Why mindfulness needs to be part of (and is not sufficient for) addressing the current societal crises

BY DUSANA DORJEE, PHD

Dusana Dorjee is a senior lecturer in psychology in education at the University of York where she leads the Well Minds Lab. Dusana authored two books on the neuroscience of meditation and co-authored a mindfulness and wellbeing school curriculum called the *Present Course*. Recently, she was a consultant on policy development for the Health and Wellbeing Areas of Learning in Wales and is an advisor for a UNESCO social and emotional learning initiative. Contact: dusana.dorjee@york.ac.uk

Chronic distractibility fuelled by the attention economy, the threat of authoritarianism, developments in artificial intelligence outpacing the ability of the human mind to adapt — these are some of the symptoms of the current and impending societal crises that are clearly and helpfully highlighted in *Mindfulness: Developing Agency in Urgent Times*. Research evidence shows that mindfulness-based training can reduce mind wandering linked to distractibility[67] and improve attention control[68] and emotional non-reactivity.[69] Hence the proposal that mindfulness has a role to play in fostering our meta-cognitive, attention and emotion-regulation abilities during the current time of constant demands on our attention is a valid one. As the paper argues, enhancing our attention and emotion regulation is likely to have a ripple effect on a more balanced decision-making. But will mindful decision-making be more altruistic? Can mindfulness make us more resilient to radical political views? Does mindfulness improve environmentally friendly behaviour? These are questions the current research doesn't provide a conclusive answer to yet, and most likely, the answer will depend on what we mean by mindfulness and how we can foster it effectively longer term.

In the Western context of mindfulness-based approaches, we often define mindfulness as purposeful non-judgmental present-moment attention.[70] Over the last two decades, the term 'mindfulness' has been increasingly used in ways that encompass additional qualities developed in traditional contemplative training such as loving-kindness, compassion or equanimity. It seems that *Mindfulness: Developing Agency in Urgent Times* uses 'mindfulness' in this widely encompassing sense, possibly interchangeably with terms such as 'meditation' or 'contemplative practice'. Subsuming a variety of contemplative practices under the same umbrella may lead to confusions about the possible effects of mindfulness.[71] For example, a programme that effectively improves attention and emotion-regulation skills via mindfulness-based training and then expands this to further develop qualities of loving-kindness, compassion and self-transcending connection to nature would be more likely to cultivate altruistic response and increase environmentally friendly behaviour than mindfulness-based training alone. We may lose sight of these differences, and the key determinants of change, if the label of 'mindfulness' becomes too widely encompassing.

This has practical implications for fostering mental capacities that could increase our individual and collective agency, particularly via education. Social-emotional learning (SEL), which has been applied in education for nearly three decades, has been aiming to support the development of knowledge and skills of attention regulation, emotion regulation, metacognition, positive goal-setting, empathy, responsible decision-making and establishing positive relationships. The latest UNESCO model of key competencies that need to be fostered by social-emotional learning is summarised as EMC2 — empathy, mindfulness, compassion and critical thinking.[72] Mindfulness is here understood in the more traditional sense as applied in mindfulness-based approaches and, together with empathy, can be considered the necessary foundation for cultivating compassion and critical inquiry. All these qualities together are likely to support the development of agency and other abilities needed for addressing the current crises.

> **Indeed, better self-regulation has been linked to better educational, wellbeing and collective outcomes such as less crime.[73] Mindfulness training can improve self-regulation[74] in children and adolescents and, in this way, support the development of their agency.**

Similarly, it has recently been suggested that the current and impending crises are particularly taxing two key mental capacities — what my work describes as the 'self-regulatory capacity' and the 'self-world capacity'.[75] The self-regulatory capacity underlies our ability to refrain from distractions and regulate our emotions and behaviour in line with our current and long-term goals. As mentioned in *Mindfulness: Developing Agency in Urgent Times*, these self-regulatory abilities contribute to our agency. Indeed, better self-regulation has been linked to better educational, wellbeing and collective outcomes such as less crime.[76] Mindfulness training can improve self-regulation[77] in children and adolescents and, in this way, support the development of their agency. In contrast, the self-world capacity is linked to our sense of self, connection with others and nature, self-focused or wider-world focused purpose in life, and so on. The self-world capacity can be developed through the cultivation of compassion,[78] self-transcending sense of purpose and prosocial activities, building on the foundations of mindfulness.

It is clear that mindfulness has the potential to contribute to addressing societal crises, even if not in the widely encompassing way suggested in *Mindfulness: Developing Agency in Urgent Times*. Possible limitations that may hinder the accomplishment of this potential need to be considered next. The current short-term focus of mindfulness-based programmes is a particularly salient challenge.[79] How many people are able and willing to practice mindfulness and develop other qualities such as compassion to the level where they would be able to harness the potential long-term benefits of these practices? What does this mean for teaching mindfulness? Where is the long-term practice of mindfulness (and other contemplative practices) to lead us? How do mindfulness-based approaches need to be developed, adapted, expanded and enhanced to accomplish this? Can we move beyond clinical focus if we emphasise standards of mindfulness teaching in clinical practice as the criterion for mindfulness teaching? Addressing these questions will likely mean closer engagement with a wider range of contemplative practices[80] and traditional contemplative ways of fostering the key capacities underlying our ability to respond mindfully, compassionately and wisely to societal crises.

So mindfulness certainly has a role to play in contributing to solutions to the current crises, particularly via fostering our capacity for self-regulation. Is mindfulness the main solution when it comes to enhancing mental capacities in the context of societal crises? That depends on how we define mindfulness, but most likely, mindfulness is an essential contributor, not a sufficient solution. Mindfulness needs to be cultivated together with empathy, compassion and critical thinking, and possibly other qualities such as a self-transcending sense of purpose, for us to effectively respond to the societal challenges. *Mindfulness: Developing Agency in Urgent Times* opens up timely discussions about the key capacities we need to cultivate urgently as part of addressing the current and impending societal crises.

RESPONSE 9

The case for compassion as another 'foundational capacity'

BY FRANCESCA BOOMSMA

Francesca Boomsma is a student with The University of Aberdeen's Mindfulness-based studies programme. Francesca has a BS in public health and teaches bilingual education, incorporating mindfulness practice in her teaching. Her other writing can be found on twitter @FBBoomsma. She has experience assisting in academic mindfulness related research projects with Temple University and Michigan Tech Institute. She is passionate about exploring the intersection of mindfulness and community wellbeing. Contact: f.boomsma.20@abdn.ac.uk

The Mindfulness Initiative's *Mindfulness: Developing Agency in Urgent Times (MDAUT)* expertly dissects the ways in which mindfulness training can encourage human agency in navigating our historical moment. The discussion paper identifies key areas in which mindfulness underpins intentional action, with Section 3.1, Interrupting automatic behaviours and choosing in the moment, particularly outlining the power in moving with this sense of purpose. Reducing reactivity, increasing self-regulation, and improving good choice-making are a few of the many mechanisms highlighted[1]. In this essay, I will broaden this argument by proposing that compassion is also a 'foundational capacity for agency'. Compassion is a powerful tool in challenging automatic behaviours, and through training, practitioners can move out of our threat-based emotional regulation system and into an improved physiological and emotional response, thereby 'replacing automatic behaviour with skill and consideration'[81]. In the most challenging of circumstances, compassion is required for us 'to live, more of the time, on purpose'.

Before research on compassion and its effects began to broaden, the word was used interchangeably with 'empathy' or 'altruism'[82]. A common working definition of compassion that the Dalai Lama provides is a 'sensitivity to the suffering of both oneself and others with a deep commitment to relieve both suffering and its causes'[83]. Other definitions of compassion include an emotion[84], a collection of skills[85], or a synonym for love[86]. Just as with mindfulness, the lack of consensual definition and differences between folk and scientific understanding make for interesting dialogues but can lead people to talk at cross-purposes. Prof. Paul Gilbert, a scholar who's spent a whole career on the subject, describes compassion as a two-fold skill that can be practised: the first step is being open and perceptive to suffering; the second includes working to prevent or relieve suffering[87]. Compassion training includes practices, techniques, and discussions that direct individuals to practise what compassion embodies: kindness, care, understanding, and connectedness.

> **In essence, compassion training, like mindfulness training, helps individuals to respond creatively rather than react blindly and to 'be more sensitive to the specific situation'[81] but always in an effort to perceive and reduce suffering.**

In essence, compassion training, like mindfulness training, helps individuals to respond creatively rather than react blindly and to 'be more sensitive to the specific situation'[81] but always in an effort to perceive and reduce suffering. It helps individuals sensitise to their environments and interrupt automatic behaviours primarily by moving us out of our threat-based emotional regulation system and into an improved physiological and emotional response.

Humans have developed three powerful emotional regulation systems[88]. The threat-based system operates on a 'better safe than sorry' basis, activating anger, anxiety, and disgust as protective responses. This fallback system represents protection and safety-seeking, despite its activating/inhibiting nature. The second system is our drive system. Here, we are driven, excited, and vitality-oriented. This system activates positive feelings and motives, pushing us to want, pursue, achieve, and consume. And somewhere perhaps in the middle of these systems lies our third: the soothing/contentment system. Here, we feel safe, connected, and restored. When we experience conflict, adversity, or suffering in our daily lives, we can more easily fall into our threat-based system. From this vantage point, it can become more difficult to gather and process information and, in turn, engage more skilfully with ourselves and others[81]. With compassion training, participants learn how to place themselves in the third soothing/contentment system by calling to action kindness, care, and common humanity. Like a muscle, learned behaviour grows stronger with practice. This learned 'healthful and skilled behaviour' models the 'intentional doing' that *MDAUT* suggests is critical in developing agency. It also circles back to self-regulation as the foundation of good choice-making.

From here, we can move towards other improved physiological changes. Compassion practices have the potential to trigger an increase of oxytocin in the brain which then activates the vagus nerve. The vagus nerve acts as a superhighway to the rest of the body, signaling an activation of the parasympathetic nervous system[89], thereby placing oneself in the soothing/contentment system. Other research in compassion training suggests lowered heart rate and a lowered inflammatory response[90]. When we move into our soothing/contentment system, we can feel the effects of compassion on our emotional state as well. Why should we feel motivated to maintain a healthy emotional state? Because the individual does not live in isolation. Emotional contagion theory posits that 'a person or group influences the emotions or behaviour of another person or group through the conscious or unconscious induction of emotion states and behavioural attitudes'[91]. Emotions are transferred. This mimicry has potential ripple effects that can close the gap between our ethical intentions and actual behaviour[81].

So how can we train? We can incorporate guided meditations and discussions centred on compassion into our individual lives, our classrooms, our boardrooms, and our political and institutional spheres. We can identify moments of adversity and choose to respond with care. As Kristen Neff outlines, we can 'attend and befriend' our difficulties in the moment, learning to be present with the inevitable struggles of life with greater ease[92]. Compassionate visualisation practices are compelling. When the brain imagines, a direct physiological response can ensue. If a hungry individual were to imagine their favourite meal, they would likely experience a physiological response of salivating and tummy rumbling. And in this way, our own thoughts can stimulate our soothing/contentment system. In compassionate visualisation, these thoughts can be highly imaginative and can take the form of people, animals, colours, or forms. Other compassion training can include meditations such as Neff's Soften, Soothe, and Allow practice.

Despite the purported benefits, it is difficult to operationalise and study compassion; turning abstract concepts into measurable observations is a challenge. Like mindfulness, some individuals who practice compassion experience unpleasant effects; opening oneself up can be scary and can invite difficult processes to work through. However, if individuals, groups, and communities incorporate compassion into their mindfulness practice — that is, actively placing themselves in a soothing/contentment system and thus improving their physiological state — they can reinforce their agency and choice in their responses.

Research into the positive effects of compassion is growing as individuals and institutions are recognizing that training is required to act well in our collective best interest, and to meet the challenges that *MDAUT* highlights. Because of its profound implications for the wellbeing of both individuals and communities, we will continue to see an upward trend of compassion practice included in the social science arena. Mindfulness training should include compassion in order to bolster intentional action and respond more effectively to life experience[81].

RESPONSE 10

The mindful reflexive self

Calling for an interdisciplinary exploration of how reflexivity and mindfulness can promote agency and social change

BY AMANDA POWELL

Amanda Powell is an independent qualitative researcher with expertise in social impact. She holds a Sociology Inequalities MSc from the University of Bristol and is a qualified mindfulness teacher. Amanda's current projects involve developing an application of reflexive mindfulness for mental wellbeing and finding meaningful work. Contact: linkedin.com/in/amanda-powell-uk

Building on the Mindfulness Initiative's 2020 report *Mindfulness: Developing Agency in Urgent Times*[93], this essay examines the largely absent sociological dimension of mindfulness as it relates to developing agency, through discussing reflexive 'internal conversation' and how this helps us make choices for the good of ourselves and society.

The essay goes on to call for a cross-disciplinary exploration of the relationship between mindfulness and reflexivity as a catalyst for social change.

What is reflexivity?

"The regular exercise of the mental ability, shared by all normal[94] people, to consider themselves in relation to their (social) contexts and vice versa... people's ability to reflect on their circumstances shapes their concerns, and in turn, influences the way they choose to act in the world" – Pioneering reflexivity researcher and Sociologist, Margaret Archer[95]

Sociological reflexivity is being aware of, and utilising, our inner voice or 'internal conversation' to inform action. As Cunliffe[96] writes, reflexivity is "finding strategies to question our attitudes, values, prejudices and assumptions to strive to understand our complex roles in relation to others. In being reflexive, we recognise we are active in shaping our surroundings, and begin critically to take circumstances and relationships into consideration".

In the COVID summer of 2020, I explored this idea by interviewing UK workers who had been recently furloughed or made redundant, to understand whether reflexivity manifested in their narratives and sense of agency. I observed that individuals seemed to use reflexivity as a tool to make sense of their situation and explore options for moving forward positively. Some were journaling in the morning, others pep-talking themselves in the mirror. Some were creating new digital networks of people who could help them, others talking about their options with friends and families and making lists of the pros and cons of moving industries. Reflexive deliberation seemed to help individuals to gain perspective, see the big picture, spot new opportunities, consider others around them and take action towards life projects. Those who disliked their relationship with their internal conversation, or avoided it altogether, described feeling somewhat lost and without agency.

In Archer's studies,[97, 98] individuals practising 'meta-reflexive deliberation (thinking about thinking) were found to be most likely to try and align their actions with benevolent values to solve issues bigger than self. So, by increasing reflexivity, we increase a person's foundational capacity for a type of agency that might equip individuals to cope with, and tackle, problems in the local community and the wider world. In my study[99] of Covid workers, meta-reflexivity seemed to help individuals make sense of their situation as part of a collective whole. Interestingly, there was some evidence that those with more limited resources and networks were less likely to demonstrate meta-reflexivity.

So, being highly reflexive seems to bring advantages individually and socially, yet academic literature is light on exploring practical solutions for how an individual with low reflexivity might develop it as a skill. This is where mindfulness enters.

How can mindfulness and reflexivity strengthen each other?

As both a reflexivity researcher and mindfulness teacher, I noticed both speak to self-awareness, perspective-taking and increasing capacity to act intentionally and for the good of society. In my study, reflexive participants often used the language of mindfulness, with themes around acceptance, non-judgment and self-compassion towards their inner voice. They spoke of an awareness of how their internal dialogue could be a friend, not a foe, in helping them cope, and vice versa. A handful of these were casual meditators but others were not. Was there a link?

More research on mindfulness as a reflexivity aid could create valuable bridges between the individual, psychological and sociological perspectives.

Reflexive mindfulness for agency in the face of inequality

The Mindfulness Initiative's 2020 report *Developing Agency in Urgent Times*[100] highlights the role of mindfulness in perspective-taking and the importance of this for individual agency:

> *"Nothing influences our ability to cope with the difficulties of existence so much as the context in which we view them. The more contexts we can choose between, the less do the difficulties appear to be inevitable or insurmountable"*

The report also states that mindfulness is a skill that can be learned by anyone, yet the sociological findings that individuals have different levels of capacity for reflexivity suggests that not everyone will be equally placed to learn mindfulness. In this respect, sociology brings to mindfulness an under-explored discussion about inequalities in individual agency. This point acknowledges the elephant in the room—that individuals in vulnerable positions face challenges that cannot be, solved by mindfulness and reflexivity. Oppressive and complex systems of inequality often weigh too heavily on an individual's agency.

Yet, as the report highlights, we must examine which levers of social change we do have the power to pull. Policy change is required to solve some of the world's most pressing issues, yet, it is individuals with the necessary agency to campaign in the streets, that help to change those policies on behalf of those who can't. The more we can prompt individuals to engage in mindful reflexive deliberation about their actions, choices and opportunities, the more we can together attack the structures that impinge on progress for social good. When it comes to tackling structural systems vs. individual agency – it is both/and not, either/or.

Summary

Mindfulness and reflexivity speak to the use of internal conversation to drive agency. Each strengthens the other and we have a lot to gain in linking them. However, while there are thousands of articles on each concept individually, there are few studies that examine the intersections.

Exploring the application of mindfulness practice as a way to increase reflexivity would fill gaps in academic debate by contributing to evidence around applied solutions. In bringing reflexivity to mindfulness, we can better examine social inequalities in people's ability to take perspectives, practice mindfulness and use their 'internal conversation' for agency. Mindfulness is sometimes criticised as the antithesis of discursive thought, inward-looking and individualistic. Linking mindfulness with reflexive deliberation helps to overcome this narrative and furthers the mindfulness for social change agenda.

To conclude, meditating or talking to ourselves out loud in the mirror won't solve the world's social issues but using mindfulness to develop reflexive self-awareness, gain perspective, connect with others and broaden the scope of social change actions we believe are within reach might be a great start. ●

Mindfulness on the frontlines

Reclaiming human sanity in the midst of torture and terror

BY RICHARD REOCH

Richard Reoch, a former trustee of the Mindfulness Initiative, was a senior representative of Amnesty International. As part of a recent high-level interfaith delegation to the Rohingya refugee camps on the Bangladesh/Myanmar border, he helped launch the Buddhist Humanitarian Project, featured by Lion's Roar in "Meditating on the Buddha in the midst of Buddhist Terror" Contact: richardreoch.info

When I was a little boy I had a three-legged wooden stool. My father would make me sit on it while he instructed me in mindfulness practice. I had no idea then what I would encounter in my life, or what a precious gift he was giving me.

I have spent years working in the realms of hatred, cruelty and extreme violence. At the same time, I have witnessed at first hand the indomitability of the human spirit. Based on my own experience – and that of accomplished practitioners I have had the honour to work with – I have seen how mindfulness practice has the power to reclaim human sanity in the midst of intense pain, disorientation and fear.

The laboratories where I have found myself putting mindfulness to the test have been places of human illegality, ill-treatment and terror. Many of my interlocutors have been the victims of horrific violence, as well as torturers and killers.

The survivors

My family was introduced to mindfulness practice by a group of survivors. They had returned from years of mass incarceration in the camps for enemy aliens throughout North America where all people of Japanese origin were detained without charge or trial during the Second World War. In the post-war years in Toronto, the painstaking reconstruction of the Japanese community included the building of a small temple they called a "Buddhist Church". Almost all of it was built by hand. My parents and I were the only non-Japanese people there for years. The hall would fall silent after the huge gong rang for meditation; and bit by bit I learned to sit still and stop swinging my legs.

Virtually the only part of the chanting that was in English was a short concluding verse in which we pledged to "labour earnestly for the welfare of all humanity." Looking back now, I can only conclude that those words must have burned themselves deeply into my young consciousness. Perhaps all the moments of sitting awkwardly in mindful silence had prepared the ground for that.

By the time I graduated from university in 1971, the Vietnam War was taking its appalling toll. The nightly news was filled with grotesque images. I began looking for somewhere I could work on the frontlines of peace.

Although the United Nations General Assembly had adopted the Universal Declaration of Human Rights in 1948, the world's human rights movement was still in its infancy. The phrase "non-governmental organization

> **I have seen how mindfulness practice has the power to reclaim human sanity in the midst of intense pain, disorientation and fear.**

(NGO)" was largely unknown. Amnesty International was one of the few. I went to London to work in their headquarters and entered the global struggle against political imprisonment and torture, executions and enforced disappearances.

Because of the nature of this work – in which I am still involved – and to protect the identities of people who are defending the victims of these abuses, it is not possible to disclose in a public journal the locations where the following encounter took place, give specific time frames, or publish the names of individuals or organizations involved.

The gift

Many years later I was part of an official delegation evaluating the work of a major international organization working to protect the victims of war. I was taken by a medical doctor to visit a secret government facility where detainees were held illegally for interrogation by the armed forces. We went into a cement block near the entrance where, once the interrogators were finished with them, the detainees were handed over to civil police authorities for release back into the community.

The doctor spoke to the officer in charge and asked to see a man who was in custody in that grey zone between the military and the police. After some time, he was brought in. He had just been tortured.

We sat down with him in silence on the cement floor. The doctor clearly knew who he was but waited a long time before asking what had happened. It was obvious that this man was not in good shape. After some time he slowly gave us a few details of what he had just been through. At one point he said, "They told me they had my wife and child. If I didn't confess, they said they would kill them. I could hear them screaming in the next room."

"That's not possible," said the doctor. "Your wife and child have been safe in my home with me all this time."

He turned towards me, a man lost in utter bewilderment, fear and personal disintegration. He was trapped between two completely contradictory realities, having no way of knowing what to believe – incapable of choosing between the screams he had heard in the nightmare of his torture, or the words of the doctor sitting on the cement in front of him.

I was at a complete loss too. I did not know this man. I had met the doctor only that morning. I knew none of the details. I was left without any idea what to think or say as this tortured being stared at me, silently screaming for help.

Then, somehow, in the midst of that horror and hopelessness, it occurred to me that there was only one thing I could try. I had no idea what effect it might have. I straightened my back as best I could and tried to relax my crossed ankles on the cement. I slightly lowered my gaze and began falteringly following my breath.

> **I had heard somewhere that it is in the bare encounter with open space that we connect with the sanity we are born with.**

I had heard somewhere that it is in the bare encounter with open space that we connect with the sanity we are born with.

At some point, he started to move. I looked up. His entire demeanour had changed. He had made his way back from delirium.

He fumbled inside his clothing, took out a crumpled little photo and handed it to me. It was his child.

For a while I cupped the picture, like a little being, in my hands. Then slowly I leaned forward and returned it to him, like a gift.

References

Why am I seeing this?
1. "The Facebook Effect" by David Kirkpatrick, page 296
2. "The Filter Bubble: What the Internet is Hiding from you" by Eli Pariser

Agency as Freedom
3. Referenced in Mindfulness: Developing Agency in Urgent Times from Schlosser, M., (2019). Agency. Stanford Encyclopaedia of Philosophy. Retrieved from: https://plato.stanford.edu/entries/agency/
4. And many have, across every field. I have particularly enjoyed works and biographies of, for example, Ludwig Wittgenstein, Iris Murdoch, Clifford Geertz, Thomas Aquinas, John Stuart Mill and Ernst Gombrich to name but a few.
5. Wikipedia provides a simple and clear definition of freedom: "the ability to act or change without constraint" Freedom – Wikipedia
6. For example, Ruth King, Rhonda Magee etc.
7. For example, Erika Carlson, Yoona Kang etc.
8. Neil Postman refers to this as 'Amusing Oneself to Death' – the title of his 1986 book.
9. Bristow, J., Bell, R., Nixon, D. (2020). Mindfulness: developing agency in urgent times. The Mindfulness Initiative. https://www.themindfulnessinitiative.org/agency-in-urgent-times/ – page 13
10. Gorringe, T.J. (2018). The World Made Otherwise – Sustaining Humanity in a Threatened World. Eugene, OR, Cascade Books. – a book poignantly dedicated to his grandchildren.
11. Ancient civilisations which held strong values, and which communicated these publicly, evidenced by their literature and laws, created impressive empires: the ancient Greeks, the ancient Chinese, Byzantium, and more recently, perhaps Victorian England.
12. If you ask the internet 'why should a business live by its values?' you will see the reach of this concept.
13. UN World Population Prospects 2019 Highlights – https://population.un.org/wpp/Publications/Files/WPP2019_Highlights.pdf
14. On the one hand, the right to education is reflected in international law in Article 26 of the Universal Declaration of Human Rights, but the content of education can be a means of control and manipulation. For example, there are significant human rights concerns about re-education camps and the inclusion of propaganda in education curricula.
15. See Freire, P. (1970). Pedagogy of the Oppressed. New York, Continuum.
16. See Arendt, H. (1958) The Human Condition. Chicago, University of Chicago Press – Arendt's theory of action describes how freedom is experienced as action and explains action as a mode of human togetherness ('plurality').

Reclaiming Sangha to transform self, society and racial injustice
17. Bristow, J., Bell, R., Nixon, D. (2020). Mindfulness: developing agency in urgent times. The Mindfulness Initiative, p 4. https://www.themindfulnessinitiative.org/agency-in-urgent-times/
18. Ibid., p 7.
19. Ibid., p 19.
20. Gleig, A. (2020) "Buddhists and Racial Justice: A History," Tricycle: The Buddhist Review, July 24. https://tricycle.org/trikedaily/buddhists-racial-justice/
21. Tuck, E., Yang, K.W. (2012) "Decolonization is not a metaphor," Decolonization: Indigeneity, Education and Society, Vol. 1, No. 1, pp 1-40.
22. Tuzzolo, E. (2016) "White Supremacy," Unitarian Universalist College of Social Justice, viewed 28 April 2021 https://uucsj.org/study-guide/legacies-of-systemic-injustice/white-supremacy
23. Bristow, J., Bell, R., Nixon, D. (2020) p 4.

24 Ibid., p 17.
25 King, R. (2018) Mindful of Race: Transforming Racism from the Inside Out. Boulder, CO.: Sounds True.
26 Bristow, J., Bell, R., Nixon, D. (2020) p 16.
27 Ibid., p 18.
28 Ibid., p 25.
29 Ibid., p 24.
30 TriCollege Libraries Research Guide, Allyship and Anti=Oppression: A Resource Guide, viewed 28 April, 2021, https://guides.tricolib.brynmawr.edu/c.php?g=285382&p=1900870
31 Ibid.
32 Sociologists such as Pierre Bourdieu and Michelle Foucault have theorised extensively power, control, individuals, and society.
33 Gleig, A. (2020)

Mindfulness in higher education

34 Ergas, O. (2017) Reconstructing 'Education' Through Mindful Attention: Positioning the Mind at the Center of Curriculum and Pedagogy. London: Palgrave Macmillan UK.
35 Barratt, C. (2014) What is contemplative pedagogy? https://contemplativepedagogynetwork.com/what-is-contemplative-pedagogy/ Accessed 22 March 2019
36 Ergas, O. and Hadar, L.L. (2019), Mindfulness in and as education: A map of a developing academic discourse from 2002 to 2017. Review of Education, 7: 757-797. DOI: 10.1002/rev3.3169
37 Arvanitakis, J. and Hornsby, D. J. (2016). Are universities redundant? In Universities, the citizen scholar and the future of higher education (pp. 7-20). Palgrave Macmillan, London.
38 Maxwell, G.A. and A. M. Broadbridge (2017) Generation Ys' employment expectations: UK undergraduates' opinions on enjoyment, opportunity and progression, Studies in Higher Education, 42:12, 2267-2283, DOI: 10.1080/03075079.2016.1141403
39 Cuijpers, P. et al. (2016). Mental disorders among college students in the World Health Organization world mental health surveys. Psychological Medicine, 46, 2955–2970. DOI: 10.1017/S0033291716001665
40 Urbina Garcia, A. (2020) What do we know about university academics' mental health? A systematic literature review. Stress and Health. 36: 563–585. https://doi.org/10.1002/smi.2956
41 Barratt, C. (2020) The Contemplative and Critical in Community. The Journal of Contemplative Inquiry. 6 (1)

The role of agency within health, and health within agency

42 Taylor, S. et al. (2019). Dependence and withdrawal associated with some prescribed medicines An evidence review. Public Health England. https://assets.publishing.service.gov.uk/government/uploads/system/uploads/attachment_data/file/940255/PHE_PMR_report_Dec2020.pdf.
43 Brine, S. and Public Health England. (2018). Prescribed medicines that may cause dependence or withdrawal. https://www.gov.uk/government/news/prescribed-medicines-that-may-cause-dependence-or-withdrawal.
44 Bristow, J., Bell, R., Nixon, D. (2020), Mindfulness: developing agency in urgent times. The Mindfulness Initiative, Sheffield, UK.
45 Nhat Hanh, T (2007). For A Future to be Possible. Parallax Press, CA.
46 Wamsler, C., Brossmann, J., Hendersson, H. et al. (2018). Mindfulness in sustainability science, practice, and teaching. Sustain Sci 13, 143–162. https://doi.org/10.1007/s11625-017-0428-2.
47 Cohen,S (2020). Psychological Vulnerabilities to Upper Respiratory Infectious Illness: Implications for Susceptibility of Coronavirus Disease 2019 (COVID-19). Association for Psychological Science https://doi.org/10.1177/1745691620942516.
48 Davidson, R.J, Kabat-Zinn, J, Schumacher, J, Rosenkranz, M, Muller, D, Santorelli, S.F, Urbanowski, F, Harrington, A, Bonus, K, Sheridan, J. F. (2003). Alterations in brain and immune function produced by mindfulness meditation. Psychosomatic Medicine, 65:564-570.
49 The Pharmaceutical Journal (2019). How pharmacists can lead the self-care revolution. DOI: 10.1211/PJ.2019.20206015.
50 Kaliman, K, Alvarez-López, M.J, Cosín-Tomás, M, Rosenkranz, M.A, Lutz, A, Davidson, R. J, (2014). Rapid changes in histone deacetylases and inflammatory gene expression in expert meditators. Psychoneuroendochrinology, 40:96-107.

51 Müller, G., Pfinder, M., Schmahl, C., Bohus, M., & Lyssenko, L. (2019). Cost-effectiveness of a mindfulness-based mental health promotion program: economic evaluation of a nonrandomized controlled trial with propensity score matching. BMC Public Health, 19(1), 1-12.

52 Watson M. C, and Neil K. E, (2019). IHPE Position Statement: Mindfulness. Lichfield: Institute of Health Promotion and Education.

53 Brewer,J.A, Mallik,S. Babuscio,T.A., Nich,C., Johnson,HE., Deleone, C.M, Minnix-Cotton, C. A. Byrne,S.A., Kober,H., Weinstein,A.J., Carroll,K.M., Rounsaville, B.J. (2011). Mindfulness training for smoking cessation: Results from a randomized controlled trial. Drug and Alcohol Dependence. Volume 119, Issues 1–2, pp 72-80. ISSN 0376-8716. https://doi.org/10.1016/j.drugalcdep.2011.05.027.

54 Bowen S, Witkiewitz K, Clifasefi S.L, Grow J, Chawla N, Hsu S.H, Carroll H.A, Harrop E, Collins S.E, Lustyk M.K, Larimer M.E. (2013). Relative efficacy of mindfulness-based relapse prevention, standard relapse prevention, and treatment as usual for substance use disorders: a randomized clinical trial. JAMA Psychiatry;71(5):547-56. doi: 10.1001/jamapsychiatry.2013.4546. PMID: 24647726; PMCID: PMC4489711.

55 Witkiewitz K, Bowen S. (2010). Depression, craving, and substance use following a randomized trial of mindfulness-based relapse prevention. J Consult Clin Psychol.;78(3):362-374. doi: 10.1037/a0019172. PMID: 20515211; PMCID: PMC3280693.

56 Carrière K, Khoury B, Günak MM, Knäuper B. (2017). Mindfulness-based interventions for weight loss: a systematic review and meta-analysis. Obes Rev. ;19(2):164-177. doi: 10.1111/obr.12623. PMID: 29076610.

57 Kang,Y, Brook O'Donnell,M, Strecher, V. J, Falk, E. B. (2016). Dispositional Mindfulness Predicts Adaptive Affective Responses to Health Messages and Increased Exercise Motivation. Mindfulness; DOI: 10.1007/s12671-016-0608-7.

58 Edwards, J. (2019). Mindfulness-based alternatives to long-term prescription drugs. The Mindfulness Initiative, Sheffield, UK.

59 Burch, V. (2009). Living Well with Pain and Illness. The mindful way to free yourself from suffering. Piatkus Books, UK.

60 Kuyken, W., Hayes, R., Barrett, B., Byng, R., Dalgleish, T., Kessler. D, Lewis, G, Watkins, E, Brejcha, C, Cardy, J, Causley, A., Cowderoy, S., Evans, A., Gradinger, F., Kaur, S., Lanham, P., Morant, N., Richards, J., Byford, S. (2015). Effectiveness and cost-effectiveness of mindfulness-based cognitive therapy compared with maintenance antidepressant treatment in the prevention of depressive relapse or recurrence (PREVENT): a randomised controlled trial. The Lancet 386 (9988) pp 63-73.

61 Coleman MT, Newton KS. Supporting self-management in patients with chronic illness. Am Fam Physician. 2005 Oct 15;72(8):1503-10. PMID: 16273817.

62 Watson, M (2008). Going for gold: the health promoting general practice. Qual Prim Care 16:177-85.

63 Watson MC and Lloyd J. (2021). Children's mental health: the UK government needs to be far more ambitious. BMJ 2021;372:n573.

64 Mindfulness All-Party Parliamentary Group (2015). Mindful Nation UK. The Mindfulness Initiative, Sheffield, UK.

65 Sapolsky RM (2004). Why Zebras Don't Get Ulcers. St. Martin's Griffin, New York.

66 Dahl CJ, Wilson-Mendenhall CD, Davidson RJ. (2020). The plasticity of wellbeing: A training-based framework for the cultivation of human flourishing. Proceedings of the National Academy of Sciences, doi: 10.1073/pnas.2014859117. Online ahead of print.

Why mindfulness needs to be part of (and is not sufficient for) addressing the current societal crises

67 Mrazek, M. D., Franklin, M. S., Phillips, D. T., Baird, B., & Schooler, J. W. (2013). Mindfulness training improves working memory capacity and GRE performance while reducing mind wandering. Psychological science, 24(5), 776-781.
Rahl, H. A., Lindsay, E. K., Pacilio, L. E., Brown, K. W., & Creswell, J. D. (2017). Brief mindfulness meditation training reduces mind wandering: The critical role of acceptance. Emotion, 17(2), 224.

68 Jha, A. P., Krompinger, J., & Baime, M. J. (2007). Mindfulness training modifies subsystems of attention. Cognitive, Affective, & Behavioral Neuroscience, 7(2), 109-119.
Kaunhoven, R. J., & Dorjee, D. (2017). How does mindfulness modulate self-regulation in pre-adolescent children? An integrative neurocognitive review. Neuroscience & Biobehavioral Reviews, 74, 163-184.

69　Paul, N. A., Stanton, S. J., Greeson, J. M., Smoski, M. J., & Wang, L. (2013). Psychological and neural mechanisms of trait mindfulness in reducing depression vulnerability. Social cognitive and affective neuroscience, 8(1), 56-64.

70　Kabat Zinn, J. (2003). Mindfulness based interventions in context: past, present, and future. Clinical psychology: Science and practice, 10(2), 144-156.

71　Dorjee, D. (2016). Defining contemplative science: The metacognitive self-regulatory capacity of the mind, context of meditation practice and modes of existential awareness. Frontiers in psychology, 7, 1788.

72　Duraiappah, A., Mercier, J., Chatterjee Singh, N. (2020). Rethinking learning: A review of social and emotional learning for education systems. Retrieved March 27, 2021 from https://mgiep.unesco.org/rethinking-learning

73　Moffitt, T. E., Arseneault, L., Belsky, D., Dickson, N., Hancox, R. J., Harrington, H., ... & Caspi, A. (2011). A gradient of childhood self-control predicts health, wealth, and public safety. Proceedings of the national Academy of Sciences, 108(7), 2693-2698.
Woodward, L. J., Lu, Z., Morris, A. R., & Healey, D. M. (2017). Preschool self regulation predicts later mental health and educational achievement in very preterm and typically developing children. The Clinical Neuropsychologist, 31(2), 404-422.

74　Pandey, A., Hale, D., Das, S., Goddings, A. L., Blakemore, S. J., & Viner, R. M. (2018). Effectiveness of universal self-regulation–based interventions in children and adolescents: A systematic review and meta-analysis. JAMA pediatrics, 172(6), 566-575.

75　Dorjee, D. (2021, March 17). The Covid-19 pandemic, political polarisation, climate change and the useless class: Why fostering wellbeing capacities should be part of the solution. https://doi.org/10.31231/osf.io/qtkyr

76　Moffitt, T. E., Arseneault, L., Belsky, D., Dickson, N., Hancox, R. J., Harrington, H., ... & Caspi, A. (2011). A gradient of childhood self-control predicts health, wealth, and public safety. Proceedings of the national Academy of Sciences, 108(7), 2693-2698. Woodward, L. J., Lu, Z., Morris, A. R., & Healey, D. M. (2017). Preschool self regulation predicts later mental health and educational achievement in very preterm and typically developing children. The Clinical Neuropsychologist, 31(2), 404-422.

77　Pandey, A., Hale, D., Das, S., Goddings, A. L., Blakemore, S. J., & Viner, R. M. (2018). Effectiveness of universal self-regulation–based interventions in children and adolescents: A systematic review and meta-analysis. JAMA pediatrics, 172(6), 566-575.

78　Weng, H. Y., Fox, A. S., Shackman, A. J., Stodola, D. E., Caldwell, J. Z., Olson, M. C., ... & Davidson, R. J. (2013). Compassion training alters altruism and neural responses to suffering. Psychological science, 24(7), 1171-1180.

79　Dorjee, D. (2017). Neuroscience and Psychology of Meditation in Everyday Life: Searching for the Essence of Mind. Routledge.

80　Ibid.

The case for compassion as another 'foundational capacity'

81　Bristow, J., Bell, R., 2020. Mindfulness: Developing Agency in Urgent Times. Mindfulness Initiative.

82　Kristeller, J. L., & Johnson, T. (2005). Cultivating loving kindness: A two stage model of the effects of meditation on empathy, compassion, and altruism. Zygon®, 40(2), 391-408.

83　Lama, D., & Rowell, G. (1995). My Tibet, Text by His Holiness the Fourteenth Dalai Lama of Tibet. University of California Press.

84　Batson, C. D., & Shaw, L. L. (1991). Evidence for altruism: Toward a pluralism of prosocial motives. Psychological inquiry, 2(2), 107-122.

85　Goetz, J. L., Keltner, D., & Simon-Thomas, E. (2010). Compassion: an evolutionary analysis and empirical review. Psychological bulletin, 136(3), 351.

86　Sprecher, S. and Fehr, B., 2005. Compassionate love for close others and humanity. Journal of social and personal relationships, 22(5), 629-651.

87　Gilbert, P., 2013. Mindful compassion: Using the power of mindfulness and compassion to transform our lives. Hachette UK.

88　Mindfulness Association (2021). University of Aberdeen MSc Studies in Mindfulness, Compassion Weekend 1 Manual, Langholm: The Mindfulness Association

89　Habib, N. (2019). Activate Your Vagus Nerve: Unleash Your Body's Natural Ability to Heal. Simon and Schuster.

90 Stellar, J.E., John-Henderson, N., Anderson, C.L., Gordon, A.M., McNeil, G.D. and Keltner, D. (2015). Positive affect and markers of inflammation: discrete positive emotions predict lower levels of inflammatory cytokines. Emotion, 15(2), 129.

91 Schoenewolf, G. (1990). Emotional contagion: Behavioral induction in individuals and groups. Modern Psychoanalysis, 15(1), 49-61.

92 Neff, K. and Sands, X. (2015). Self-compassion: The proven power of being kind to yourself. New York, NY: William Morrow.

The mindful reflexive self

93 Bristow, J. Bell, R. Nixon, D. Developing Agency in Urgent Times. 2020. The Mindfulness Initiative. Report accessed online here: https://www.themindfulnessinitiative.org/agency-in-urgent-times

94 Regarding Archer's use of the word 'normal'. In her 2007 book, 'Making our way through the world, Archer states that 'normal' refers to individuals without cognitive impairment or psychological mental health disorders – this essay acknowledges that this word is problematic.

95 Archer, M. S. (2007) Making our way through the world: human reflexivity and social mobility. Cambridge, UK: Cambridge University Press.

96 Cunliffe, A.L. (2009a) Reflexivity, learning and reflexive practice, (Chap23) in S. Armstrong and C. Fukami (eds), Handbook in Management Learning, Education and Development. London: Sage

97 Archer, M. S. (2007) Making our way through the world: human reflexivity and social mobility. Cambridge, UK: Cambridge University Press

98 Archer, M. S. (2012) The reflexive imperative in late modernity. New York: Cambridge University Press.

99 Powell, A. 2020. "A qualitative exploration of Archer's reflexivity and work during the 2020 COVID-19 pandemic" – Qualitative study as part of Sociology MSc dissertation. University of Bristol. Unpublished.

100 Bristow, J. Bell, R. Nixon, D. Developing Agency in Urgent Times. 2020. The Mindfulness Initiative. Report accessed online here: https://www.themindfulnessinitiative.org/agency-in-urgent-times